SUCCESSFUL CAR BUYING

SUCCESSFUL CAR BUYING.

How to come out a winner,
whether you buy new, buy used, or lease

Steve Ross

Illustrations by Larry Fink

Stackpole Books

Published by
STACKPOLE BOOKS
Cameron and Kelker Streets
P.O. Box 1831
Harrisburg, PA 17105

Printed in the United States of America

10 9 8 7 6 5 4 3 2 1

First Edition

Cover and interior illustrations © Larry Fink
Cover design by Tracy Patterson

Library of Congress Cataloging-in-Publication Data

Ross, Steve, 1958–
    Successful car buying : how to come out a winner, whether you buy new, buy used, or lease / Steve Ross. – 1st ed.
        p.   cm.
    ISBN 0-8117-2246-5 : $8.95
    1. Automobiles – Purchasing. I. Title.
    TL162.R68   1990   89-35283
    629.222 – dc20   CIP

To Mimi for her patience, understanding, encouragement, and moral support.

Contents

Introduction

Are you tired of your car? Is your family outgrowing it? Perhaps your job or recreational activities requires a different kind of vehicle. People buy cars for many reasons. What are yours? Realize that some may be emotional. Understanding your reasons and needs prepares you to buy rationally.

You have taken the first step toward rational buying by purchasing this unique and concise handbook, written by someone with years inside the car business. With this step-by-step consumer awareness guide you will have more confidence and knowledge about car buying and more power in negotiating – and you will end up with more money in your pocket.

1   *Planning Ahead*

The Basics

Always remember that YOU are the customer and it is YOUR money. Buy what YOU want! Purchasing a car is a long-term investment, not to be taken lightly. Make sure you choose the automobile you want to live with. This means liking the way it drives, not just the way it looks. An excellent approach is to envision yourself in the car during your ordinary life situations. If you can picture yourself in that car, then it is probably the one for you.

Needs

Before you go *near* a car lot, you should decide what type of car you are looking for. Make a list of your needs. Think about how you will use the car. What do you and/or your family need the car to do? Do you want a sporty car for weekend drives on the open road? Do you need the vehicle mainly for business purposes? Will you often have many passengers? Do you want two or four doors . . . a station wagon . . . a hatchback . . . automatic or manual transmission . . . air-conditioning . . . power steering . . . power windows . . . power door locks . . . power brakes . . . stereo . . . sunroof?

For example, suppose Mr. Perez is a thirty-two-year-old government worker with a wife and two small children. He needs a car mainly for work and family purposes. He needs room to carry cargo and wants economical, dependable transportation.

Based on this profile, Mr. Perez clearly does not want a two-seat sports car! Because he needs room for family and cargo, a large sedan or station wagon would be best. A two-door vehicle would be inconvenient. As to features, air-conditioning and power steering would make for comfort and easy handling. Child safety locks and driver controlled windows are also important features for families with small children. As you can see, careful consideration of your needs will help assure a proper purchase.

Do not *ever* rush to make your purchase. Remember to create a picture of the car you want before visiting any car dealers.

Where Do You Go?

Ideally, you want to purchase the car from a local dealer, to save time now and for convenient servicing later. Nevertheless, do not limit your search to local dealers – the convenience of buying locally could be costly if a better deal exists fifteen or twenty miles away. Buying your car away from home does not prevent you from servicing locally; it is common to buy in one place and service at another. Buy from the dealer who gives the best deal, even if that dealership is not close to home. Recommendations from friends and previous customers can help; consulting your local Better Business Bureau and consumer protection agencies (for consumer complaints) is another good idea.

Is There a Best Time to Buy?

This may sound strange, but actually there IS a best time of day and month to buy. When? Shortly before closing time on the last day of the month. The dealership always wants one more sale by month's end. Selling cars is a straight commission job; if there is no sale, there is no money for the salesperson. To create excitement for that last extra sale, the dealership generally has a bonus program. Since the manager and salesperson have an extra incentive, you usually will not get the same deal any other time of the month. Shop first (you'll learn how in upcoming chapters), then come in to close the deal at the end of the month.

Summary:
1. Understand your needs. Create a picture of the car that best suits your needs and preferences.
2. Buy from the dealer who gives the best deal, even if that dealership is not close to home.
3. The best time to buy is shortly before closing time on the last day of the month.

2   *Face to Face*

The Car Lot

Now that you have made your list of needs and have the picture of your car fixed firmly in mind, it is time to visit the dealerships. DO NOT SIGN ANYTHING until you have been to at least three dealerships. Be ready to compare models, prices, and services in order to get the best deal.

Ideally, when you step onto the car lot, you will be greeted by a friendly, informative, and non-threatening salesperson. If you do not like the salesperson, simply ask for someone else; *do not let yourself be intimidated.* If the salesperson asks why, just say you would prefer someone more cooperative. If there is still an objection, state that "half a commission is better than none." (In the automobile industry, it is common practice for commissions to be split if more than one salesperson has to get involved in the sale.) Remember, you are the customer and the salespeople are there to serve you. They want your money; you can — and should — use that leverage to your advantage.

Once you have found a salesperson who is friendly and informative, you are ready to proceed.

Just because a salesperson offers to sell you a car "at invoice (the price the dealer paid the manufacturer for the vehicle) or below" does not mean you are getting the best deal. The words "at or below invoice" are a gimmick. The manufacturer usually gives the dealer a rebate or other incentive, making the real cost to the dealer less than the invoice price.

The Manufacturer's Sticker

Every new car on the lot has a factory sticker glued onto the window. This sticker is not put on by the dealer; it is put on by the manufacturer. The manufacturer's sticker tells you two things. First, it lists the standard equipment, such as engine size, type of transmission, rear-window defogger. Second, it states the suggested retail price.

Occasionally you will find a second sticker on the window, put there by the dealer. This is called an addendum sticker; it lists any "aftermarket" items added by the dealer. Common aftermarket items are alarms, pinstriping, luggage racks, paint sealant (also called paint undercoat), and special wheels. The dealer then adds the manufacturer's sticker to the dealership's sticker for the total price of the car. *This total price has a lot of built-in profit. If you pay this price, you are paying too much.* For instance, dealers may charge $125 for pinstriping when it costs them $25, or $795 for an alarm that costs $250. (In addition, car alarms installed by dealers may be of poor quality.)

Generally, dealers do not want to remove factory equipment such as a stereo, or dealer installed items like pinstriping. They would rather discount an item than re-move it.

When you visit dealerships, try to copy down everything on the factory and dealer stickers. Doing this makes it eas-ier to compare prices from dealer to dealer. Your visits should be geared toward deciding which car(s) best fits your needs.

There are also books like *Edmund's New Car Prices* and the *Kelley Blue Book* that provide standard costs for cars and optional items. Bookstores, libraries, and banks gener-ally have these books.

Summary:
1. Find a friendly and informative salesperson.
2. If you pay the dealer's asking price, you are paying too much.
3. Compare prices, including aftermarket items, from at least three dealerships.

3   *Show and Tell*

The Sales Presentation

The sales presentation consists of an explanation of the car's features and, more importantly, a road test. Remember, taking a demo ride and listening to a salesperson do not commit you to buying. Be sure to compare the picture of the car you created earlier to the car you are being shown now. Make sure *you* touch everything *yourself.* Get involved!

The salesperson will use a presentation technique called the assumptive approach, which means taking you as far as you will go toward the final sale. *The salesperson will act as if you want to buy this car now,* and it is up to you to stop him. He will go from explaining the features of the car to the demo ride to the discussion of financing to signing the papers; if you give in to each step, you may be sold a car you do not want. You must remain firm in refusing to be "sold" right on the spot.

The Demo Ride

Once you have selected the car that best fits your picture and listened to the sales presentation, you should take a demonstration ride. Remember, taking a demo ride does not commit you to anything.

Generally, the salesperson drives the car onto the street because the dealership's insurance policy does not cover a customer driving off the lot. Also, before you get into your demonstration car, you may be asked to present your driver's license. (This protects you, the dealership, and the salesperson in case of an accident.) Show it, but keep it in your wallet — never give your license or registration to dealership personnel. It is surprisingly common for a customer who is unfamiliar with the car to suffer the shock and embarrassment of a "little accident" on a test drive. If it happens to you, the dealership is fully insured and you are not obligated to buy the car. Just tell the dealer to notify their insurance company. If they give you any trouble, call the police to report the accident and get the salesperson off your back.

When it is your turn to drive, the salesperson will usually sit in the front passenger seat. This position gives him more control over your driving and allows him to continue the "pitch." But if you are a couple, or have a friend with you, put your companion up front and the salesperson in the back. The salesperson should not be insulted by the request. If you are a couple, make sure you both drive.

Dealerships have specific routes for test drives. Tell them you want to drive under your own conditions, however. They should be happy to accommodate you because they want to make a sale. You should drive under your conditions because only you know what sort of driving you do. Try driving up hills, with and without the air-conditioning, to check the car's power. A spin on the freeway (if one is nearby) is also important to check acceleration and high-speed handling. Park on a private street and look at the car from a distance. The car will look different in a realistic setting than it did surrounded by dozens of similar cars.

Most test drives last fifteen to thirty minutes, but do not feel pressured for time. Remember, it is your money, you are the customer.

When you return from your demo ride, the salesperson may ask you to park in the "sold line." Don't worry, parking there does not make a sale – you have not bought a car until you sign a sales contract. There is really no such thing as a sold line; it is just another step in the assumptive sales approach. The salesperson is testing your reaction. Remember, he will push the sale as far as possible. His goal is to get you to buy now. Your goal is to get the best deal, now or later!

Summary:
1. Take a test drive, under your conditions, suitable for your kind of driving.
2. Park on a private street and look at the car from a distance.
3. Do not feel pressured for time.
4. You do not buy a car until you sign on the dotted line.

Role Play One

There is a right way and a wrong way to go through the initial sales presentation and test drive we've just described. Unfortunately, many people are unprepared, disorganized, and passive, giving the salesperson control of the situation. Let's take a look at the wrong way first, then the right way, putting the principles we have outlined into action.

(S = Salesperson and C = Customer)

S: Hi! Welcome to Happy Motors. How can I help you?

C: Oh, I'm just looking . . . not doing any buying.

(This response is an attempt to avoid the sales pitch. It does quite the opposite, however, by allowing the salesperson to take charge of the conversation.)

S: OK . . . but what did you have in mind . . . a two door . . . four door?

(Notice how the salesperson is using the assumptive approach, completely ignoring your objections.)

C: Well, like I said, I won't be buying today.

S: That's fine. What kind of car do you drive now?

(The salesperson starts asking a list of questions, called "qualifying questions," to discover your financial situation and the type of car you are looking for.)

C: A four door.

S: Well, follow me and let me show you some of our four doors.

C: OK.

(The salesperson is literally leading the customer around.)

S: When you bought your last car did you buy it from a local dealer, or far away? Did you pay cash or finance it?

(These questions seek to discover whether you shop around and whether you have established credit.)

C: (Most customers answer these questions quickly and truthfully, allowing the salesperson to size up the cus tomer.)

S: What are you looking for in a car?

(This question seeks to discover the size and features of your desired car.)

C: Well, I need an automatic transmission, air-conditioning, power steering, power windows, and a nice stereo system.

S: Do you prefer light or dark colors?

(By asking about general tones rather than specific colors, the salesperson can suggest whatever light or dark color is on the lot. This tactic prevents the customer from naming only one color, which may not be available.)

C: Uh . . . light colors.

S: Great, let me show you what we have here.

C: OK.

(As you are shown a car, look for other cars on the lot that *you* like.)

S: By the way, is there anyone else who will be helping you in the selection?

(This question gauges the chances of making a sale now by discovering whether another person is involved in the buying decision. If the answer is no, you have informed the salesperson that you are the decision maker, allowing for a sale now.)

C: Well yes . . . my wife/husband.

(This answer requires a different sales approach.)

S: And where are they right now?

(The salesperson is setting you up to drive the car to your spouse *now*.)

C: At work.

S: Does your spouse know that you're out shopping for a car now?

(If you say yes, the salesperson considers you a buyer, as both decision makers have agreed to buy a car; if you say no, the salesperson believes the sale will be more difficult, as another person must also be "sold.")

C: Well . . . yes.

S: Well, let's visit them at their job right now and let them have a drive too.

(If you say yes, the salesperson will want to visit your spouse now. If you say no, the salesperson will keep trying to sell you, hoping *you'll* sell your partner.)

C: No, no! Remember, I told you I'm not buying today!

S: I understand that, but if you like the car and the price is right, why can't we make a deal?

C: Well, I'd have to call and find out.

(This response shows that the salesperson is dominating the customer. Again, be firm in refusing to be "sold" right away.)

S: What's your spouse's work number?

(This is an attempt to get the other decision maker involved in the sale now. The salesperson will either drive to the spouse's job or have the spouse visit the dealership immediately.)

C: Now is not a good time to call.

S: All right, let's go for a test drive in the car you want to
    buy.

(The salesperson is still in assumptive mode and cannot
hear the word "no.")

C: OK.

(This response allows the salesperson to continue the sales
pitch. Remember, you can leave at any time.)

S: I'll need to see your driver's license for insurance pur-
    poses, and I'll drive the car off the lot.

C: OK.

S: Now it's your turn.

(You get behind the wheel and are asked to follow the
regular dealership route. However, you should drive under
your conditions, since only you know the type of driving
you do. After fifteen to thirty minutes you return to the
dealership lot.)

S: OK, pull over there and park in the sold line.

(There is no such thing as a sold line. This is an imaginary
area, created by the salesperson's desire to sell. If you park
in the sold line you have not agreed to buy the car.)

C: What do you mean the "sold line"? I told you before I'm
    not buying today!

S: I understand you're not buying.

C: I should hope so.

S: Turn the engine off and follow me.

C: OK.

(Notice how the salesperson is continuing on to the next step in the sale. The customer keeps following him around.)

Now, consider that scene. You can see how the salesperson had total control, despite the customer's objections. *Salespeople do not hear the word no.* Their only goal is to have you sign on the dotted line. Remember, do not sign ANYTHING until you have selected the exact car you want and negotiated with three dealerships.

Controlling the Sales Presentation

Gaining and maintaining control of the sales presentation is actually quite simple. The golden rule is ORGANIZATION.

Let's do that role play again. This time, the customer will be in control of the sales presentation.

S: Hi! Welcome to Happy Motors. How can I help you?

C: Well, let me tell you about the type of car I want. First of all, I need a four door with an automatic transmission. The basic features I need are air-conditioning, power windows, power steering, and power brakes. Also a cloth interior and a light exterior color. I won't need a stereo system since I'll be installing my own.

(Notice how the customer takes charge of the buying situation immediately by describing the size and features desired. This prevents the salesperson's assumptive approach. You are not answering probing questions; instead, you are quickly in charge of the conversation.)

S: I have just what you described. By the way, how much are you going to spend?

(This question seeks the price range of cars for this customer. The salesperson does not want to demonstrate a car that the customer cannot afford.)

C: At this time price has not entered my mind.

(Notice the customer evading the salesperson's attempt to gain control of the sales presentation.)

S: Why is that?

C: Because I'm not buying now. All I want to do is select a car.

S: OK.

(The salesperson shows you the selection. If you do not like any of the cars you are shown, it is time to leave. If you find a car you like, continue to the next step.)

S: Let's go for a test drive.

C: Here's my driver's license. And please mention to your manager that we will be gone a little longer than usual, because I don't want to drive your regular demo route. I would like to drive under my normal everyday conditions. Please make sure there's plenty of gas.

S: Everything is fine.

C: I'd appreciate it if you would sit in the back seat. I'd feel more comfortable with my friend/spouse up front.

S: I'll get in the back seat in a moment. I've got to drive the car off the lot due to insurance requirements.

C: Thank you!

(Once on the street, you drive the car as you would in your everyday conditions, and then return to the dealership.)

C: OK, let's go back.

S: Be careful when you pull onto the lot. Please park in the sold line over there (pointing).

C: On the condition that you understand I'm not buying today.

(Notice that the customer is in total control, *giving instructions,* not answering questions.)

S: That's OK. Please turn the engine off and follow me (into the showroom).

C: OK.

You can now distinguish the difference between you controlling the sales presentation and the salesperson controlling it. When you are in control (by being organized), you get all the information you need to make a decision while preventing a sale by the assumptive approach.

Summary:
1. If you find yourself answering questions, you are not in control.
2. If you find yourself giving a lot of information, such as whether your spouse makes the decisions, you are not in control.
3. When you give directions, you are in control.
4. When you are shown the types of cars you want without being led around, you are in control.

4   *"Is This Your Choice?"*

Dealer Stock vs. Dealer Trade

Often the dealer does not have the exact car you want on the lot. Perhaps the desired color, or a particular feature, is lacking in the cars that are in stock. The most widely heard comment customers make to salespeople is, "The car is just missing something." This may be the difference between making or breaking a deal for the dealer. Under these circumstances, the dealer may tell you: "You can have the exact car you want, but we will have to do a dealer trade." This means that two dealers trade one car for another. Occasionally you will have to wait a day or two to get your selected car.

In this situation, the customer is usually required to leave a large deposit. Do not be surprised if the dealer wants $500 or more. Sometimes they will say your deposit is non-refundable. THIS IS NOT TRUE. It most certainly *is* refundable! This is just a scare tactic to get a definite commitment from you to buy now.

They want to take you out of the market, because a dealer trade gives you time to reconsider the deal and visit other dealerships. The dealer is thinking: "If I cannot get your money *now*, then I am wasting my time doing a dealer trade."

You will probably get a better deal when the dealership can avoid doing a trade. The trade requires extra time and effort for the dealer, and they want a sale now. If you present the dealer with a choice of selling a car in stock for a large discount versus doing all the work that a dealer trade requires, the dealer will choose the sale now. In any event, the dealer will not tell you where your exact car is located. If they did, you could go to that other dealer and buy the car there.

Bumping

Customers frequently cannot buy the cars they really want. Why? They are too expensive. If the dealer senses that you are a buyer (someone who wants a car now but cannot afford the "pictured model"), they will try to switch you to a less expensive new car. This is called bumping. The suggested car will usually be quite similar to the first choice. If price is still a problem, they will bump again, to a similar used car.

The term "bumping" is used widely in the auto industry. It means switching the customer to something he does not want, whether it is a different car model or a higher monthly payment. During these emotionally charged moments, make sure you are not pressured into buying something you will come to regret later. Remember to keep fixed firmly in your mind the picture of your car.

Demos

While not typical new cars, demonstrators are also for sale. Demos are the cars used for test drives, and they are also given to salespeople and managers for personal use. The advantage to buying a demo is price. The disadvantages are that demos have been driven, often a few thousand miles, and usually not with the utmost care. The balance of the manufacturer's warranty still applies to a demo, and extended service contracts (discussed in more detail in chapter 7) are available.

The price break on a demo varies, but beware, dealers try to make up for this discount on other parts of the deal. For example, higher interest rates, fancy paint jobs, and other accessories are pushed on the customer to offset the lower price of the demo. Remember to keep your eyes on the "extras."

Dealers must disclose that a car is a demo. Many state laws even require the customer to sign a special statement indicating they've been told the car is a demo. Know what you are buying, a brand new car or a demo.

Summary:

1. In dealer trades, the customer is usually required to leave a large deposit. Remember, deposits are refundable.
2. Better deals are likely when the dealership can avoid doing a trade.
3. Recognize when you are being bumped. Make sure you are not pressured into buying something you will regret later.
4. Price is the advantage in buying a demo, but watch out for costly extras.
5. A dealer must disclose that a car is a demo.

5   *Creative Financing*

Financing Options

Once you've found the best match with that mental picture of your ideal car, you're ready to start negotiating for the best price possible for that car. Unless you're one of the fortunate people who can pay cash for the car, financing will be a critical part of the negotiations. Understanding financing is crucial in your negotiations with the dealer.

Even if you can pay cash, you may prefer to finance the car with an auto loan. If you can earn a higher rate of interest on your personal savings than you'll pay for the auto loan, consider keeping your savings in the bank.

The key issue in financing is: how much can you afford? That's something only you can decide. You must assess how much you can spend for monthly payments, and how much you're willing to pay for the total price of the car.

You will want to negotiate all the aspects of financing, such as the size of the down payment, the amount of the loan, the interest rate, and the size of the monthly payment. These are all parts of the total cost of the car. A successful buyer negotiates the total price, then works out the financing. You must discuss financing terms fully with each of the three dealers you visit in order to get a meaningful price quote on the car you want.

Some car buyers arrange their own financing through a bank or credit union, and usually get a lower interest rate than dealers offer. Banks might not finance people with borderline credit, however. In these instances, the dealer may be the only way to get financed. Dealers generally borrow money through finance companies, which take weaker credit but charge higher interest rates.

A buyer may not have strong enough credit to finance a car. In that case, the lender may request a co-signer, a second party to guarantee repayment of the loan. If the obligation to pay is not fulfilled, the co-signer is responsible as if he or she were the buyer. If a co-signer is needed to assist the purchase, the interest rate will be a lot higher, as the risk is greater. Think twice if you need a co-signer. (Think three times if someone asks you to be his co-signer!) The co-signer assumes a big responsibility.

Rules for co-signers vary from bank to bank and dealer to dealer. For example, the buyer may be allowed only a parental co-signer, mother or father. Some lenders accept home owners whether related or not. Others accept any blood relative, such as an aunt, uncle, or other family member.

Dealer Finance

Do not be seduced by "zero percent financing" or other low interest rates offered by manufacturers. Banks don't offer very low interest rates because they would not make a profit. Manufacturers, however, can offer interest rates such as 2.9%, 2.4%, or even 0% because they make their money in other ways. Remember, the dealer knows many tricks to compensate for low interest rates or other "breaks" you think you're getting.

Few customers qualify for these preferred rates. As stated in the advertisements, restrictions do apply. In order to get that low interest rate the manufacturer may require a larger down payment than usual and/or offer a shorter finance period, such as twenty-four or thirty-six months. This shorter term means a higher monthly payment than forty-eight- or sixty-month financing, but if you need long-term financing, the interest rate will be a lot higher than the "special" rate.

Buy Rate

When the dealer arranges financing, one very important trick they use is making money from the buy rate. The dealer will arrange a loan for a rate several points higher than the lender is actually charging. For example, if the dealer arranges financing for 16% but actually borrowed that money at 8%, they doubled the total finance charges. The lender's interest rate – the buy rate – is half what the dealer charged.

The lender sends the dealer the extra interest that the dealer charged the customer. This translates into thousands of dollars in profit for the dealer! There is no profit from the buy rate when you arrange your own financing, because you know the actual interest rate.

Financing Charts

Three factors determine your monthly payment and the total price of the car: the amount of money you borrow, the interest rate on the loan, and the length of the loan. In order to show the interaction between these factors, we've provided financing charts at the end of the book. These charts give the monthly payment amounts at selected interest rates (8¾%, 12¾%, and 16¾%). They are provided for comparative purposes, so that you'll be comfortable dealing with the numbers and have a rough idea of how different rates and repayment periods affect the total finance charge. Complete charts for all interest rates can be found in your local library and many bookstores.

To illustrate how to use the monthly loan payment charts, let's suppose Mrs. Russell wants to buy a car that costs $15,000. She has a down payment of $3,000; she therefore wants a loan for $12,000. To find her monthly payments for a five-year (sixty-month) loan at 8¾% interest, locate the chart for that interest rate, look down the left side of the page to find the $12,000 line, and read across to the Five Years column. The monthly payment is $247.65. Look to the left of the Five Years column and you'll see that if Mrs. Russell can repay the loan in two years, she'll make a monthly payment of $546.84.

Which is the better deal? The one Mrs. Russell can afford. The higher the monthly payment you can afford, the lower the finance charge, and thus the lower the total price of the car. That's the best deal. But if you can't afford the monthly payment, stretching the length of the loan will decrease it. The extra finance charges may be worthwhile if that lower monthly payment lets you purchase the car that fits your picture.

In addition to the length of the loan, the interest rate is

crucial to the monthly payments and the total cost of the loan. If Mrs. Russell has to borrow her $12,000 at 12¾% instead of 8¾% (still for sixty months), the chart shows she'll pay $271.50 monthly. That's almost $25 dollars a month more than the payment for the loan at the lower rate. Over the sixty-month repayment period, it adds up to an additional finance charge of $1,431—that's an extra $1,431 added to the total price of her car.

Mrs. Russell can also save on both the monthly payment and finance charge by increasing the down payment, either by negotiating a better price for the new car or for her trade, or by putting down more cash. Reducing the amount of the loan from $12,000 to $11,000 will save her $20 per month in payments (that's $1,200 over sixty months).

If you have a certain monthly payment in mind, you can use these charts to identify the different loan amounts and terms you can expect to pay. This will give you a better idea of your price range. For example, if your budget tells you that you can afford a monthly payment of $300, the chart shows that at 8¾% you can borrow about $3,500 for one year, $6,500 for two years, $9,500 for three years, $12,000 for four years, or $14,500 for five years. At a 16¾% interest rate, the chart shows that the amounts you can borrow for a $300 monthly payment are significantly lower and the finance charges are much higher. Even over five years, you can't borrow much more than $12,000, and so you won't be able to afford some cars that would be within your reach at a lower interest rate.

Before you start negotiating with a dealer, get comfortable with the basic principles of financing and understand the relationship between the total cost of the loan (principal plus finance charges), the monthly payment, the interest rate, and the length of the loan. You'll avoid falling prey to many of the salesperson's tricks and save yourself thousands of dollars in finance charges over the repayment period.

Time Is Money

Two factors affect how much you pay in finance charges: how much money you borrow (the loan amount) and how long you borrow it for (the loan term).

Customers are happy when the dealership offers thirty days, forty-five days, or even sixty days until the first payment. This extra time raises each monthly payment a few dollars, for the term of the loan. The customer pays for that first extra month or two for the next several years!

On the other hand, if you repay the loan early, you're entitled to an interest refund. The loan will be re-calculated and interest charged only for the period of time you actually borrowed the money. A quick way to pay off a loan early is to make two payments at once for a few months; within a short period of time you will be far ahead. These are general rules that apply to all loans, whether financed through a bank or the dealer.

Time is interest, meaning more profit for the lender. So more time is, literally, more money!

Summary:

1. Know what you can afford to pay for a car before negotiating with any dealer.
2. Understand how the interest rate, amount of money borrowed, and length of repayment term affect the total price of the car. Know the financing options that fit your budget.
3. Think twice if you need a co-signer. If the lender wants a co-signer, it indicates the loan may be too much for you to handle.

4. Don't be seduced by advertised low interest rates, which often carry restrictions on the length of the loan or down payment required. Not everyone qualifies for these preferred rates.

6   *Negotiating*

Basic Information

Now that you have selected the exact car pictured in your mind, know how much you can afford to spend, and understand the basics of financing, it is time to negotiate the price and terms of your deal. Remember that throughout the negotiations, you are not committed to buy the car.

Role Play Two

There is a right way and a wrong way to negotiate; the golden rule is "Preparation and Comparison." Unfortunately, many people are unprepared, disorganized, and passive, giving the salesperson control. Let us demonstrate the wrong way, and then the right way.

S: Aren't you excited about your new car? (Customer usually agrees.) Well, you'll be driving it real soon.

Let's start the paperwork. How do you want your new car registered? In your name only, or yours and your husband's/brother's/daughter's name?

(A classic example of the "assumptive approach." This question is geared toward having the customer believe they've already bought that car.)

C: I don't understand.

S: Do you want the new car titled the same as your old registration? The same name, address, city, and zip code?

C: Wait a minute, I'm not buying.

S: But it's necessary to get this information to give you a price.

(The salesperson will eventually give a price without this information. This ploy is part of the standard operating procedure to make you believe that you are buying this car.)

C: (States information.)

S: Thank you. OK now, your car is a Subaru GL sedan, with an automatic transmission, stock number 395. (The stock number lets the dealership identify the car from its inventory.) The car you're trading in is a 1981 Datsun 200SX five-speed with 65,000 miles. Do you own your car now?

C: Yes.

S: Where is the pink slip? (The pink slip is the ownership title.)

(If a customer visits a car lot with the pink slip, this identifies him as a buyer ready to trade in his old car. If a

deal occurs without the pink slip, the dealer has the customer sign a document stating the pink slip will be sent
immediately.)

C: Right here.

S: Did you finance your car last time?

(This question seeks to discover your credit history.)

C: Yes.

S: What were your monthly payments and how long a
term was the loan for?

C: $250 per month for sixty months.

S: OK, the price of the new car is $13,000, plus sales tax
and license fees.

(Sales tax is not charged on the license fees. That charge
goes to the Department of Motor Vehicles for the registration of your new car.)

C: I don't want to pay $13,000.

S: No problem, I'm on your side. Let me just continue and
we'll work out a price later.

(The salesperson is trying to divert your attention from the
bottom line.)

S: For a preferred financing rate, the bank requires one-
third of the selling price as a down payment. One-third
of $13,000 is $4,330. That's not a problem for you, is it?

C: I didn't want to put down more than $2,500. Also, what
about my trade?

S: Oh, we'll get to that later.

(The salesperson has already appraised your trade, but will

avoid making an offer. Most customers ask more for the trade than the dealer offers. The dealer does not want to offend a customer early in the negotiations by making a low offer. Therefore, the salesperson tries to quickly brush your questions aside and continue with the sales attempt.)

S: Based on $2,500 down – that's what you wanted to put down, right?

(Notice how you are led along. You mention a preference and the salesperson converts it to fact, making your preference part of the sales pitch. Your own words come back to haunt you.)

C: Right.

S: Your monthly payment is only $450 per month for thirty-six-month financing!

(These numbers are made up. High numbers are often mentioned; they are designed to shock the customer. They make the smaller numbers, like $300 per month, sound like a bargain.)

C: That's too high! I only wanted payments of $230 per month for forty-eight months!

S: It's OK . . . I'm on your side. Besides, I know my manager wants to make a deal, so let's work further.

C: What about my trade?

S: We'll talk about that just as soon as you OK your offer of $230 per month for forty-eight months so I can submit it to management.

C: OK. (Signs offer sheet.)

(Agreeing to and even signing this offer of $230 for forty-eight months is not binding. What the salesperson really wants to do is have you commit to some terms, from which you can be bumped in upcoming negotiations. This also pushes you into a negotiating mode.)

S: Thank you, I'll take this to the sales manager and be right back.

(After a short absence the salesperson returns.)

S: My manager says your figures are unrealistic, but we are close. Also, we can offer you $1,500 for your trade.

(The salesman has this customer committed to $230 per month for forty-eight months; he now wants to discuss down payment. As the trade-in and the down payment are interrelated, the trade-in value now becomes important for the dealer. This is especially true if the customer wants the trade as the only form of down payment.)

C: My car is worth $2,500.

S: Let me show you why it's only worth $1,500. Follow me.

(The salesperson takes the customer to the trade-in vehicle and picks out all the problems: the bad paint job, the torn upholstery, the bald tires, the worn-out carpet, anything and everything that needs to be fixed. The salesperson then totals the damage at a high figure, and states that your car would be worth your figure, except for the damage, which adds reconditioning costs.)

S: You said you wanted to put down $2,500, right? But your car is only worth $1,500. However, we can work the deal so you can use your trade as the down payment with no cash needed. Isn't that great?

(The dealer makes the customer feel good by accepting the trade as the down payment.)

C: If you will take the car as the down payment, we are OK.

(Now that the customer is committed to a down payment, the salesperson returns to the monthly payments.)

S: OK. About those monthly payments, $230 per month is not possible with only the trade-in as the down payment. We'll need $340 per month, for forty-eight months.

(Again, these numbers are made up. They make the smaller numbers sound like a bargain.)

C: I can't afford that, it's just too high.

S: Well, we can lower that monthly payment to $315 if we go to sixty months.

(This is a good example of bumping. The customer originally offered $230 for forty-eight-month financing, but is now being talked into $315 per month for sixty-month financing.)

C: I can go to $260 per month for sixty months.

S: I'll take your offer to my manager.

(During this absence, the salesperson's discussion with the manager goes something like this: S = Salesperson and M = Manager)

S: I can get this guy's trade for $1,500, and he insists on no cash down and is now at $260 per month for sixty months.

M: Well, we appraised the trade at $2,500, too. That's the actual cash value. We're offering $1,500, so we just made $1,000 on the trade. Now bump him to $285 and we'll make the deal. ($285 for sixty months equals a total payment of $17,100, on financing $11,500 at 16¾%.)

(The salesperson now returns to the customer.)

S: Congratulations, you've got a deal—at $285.

Who had control of this buying situation? The salesperson! Even when the customer had objections, the salesperson continued on as though those objections did not exist.

Here's how YOU can be in control. Remember, it is *your money.*

Let's pick it up from where the salesperson first mentions price.

S: OK, the price of the new car is $13,000, plus sales tax and license fees.

C: I don't want to pay $13,000.

S: No problem, I'm on your side. Let me just continue and we can talk about price later.

C: Well, if you're on my side, let me tell you exactly what offer I want you to submit to your manager.

(Take control. Use the salesperson's words against him.)

S: OK.

C: I don't want to pay the sticker price of $13,000. But I'm reasonable. I realize that you have to make a living, too. (It's good to empathize with the salesperson. You can be just as cunning as he is.) I want 30% off the asking price.

S: OK. I'll write that down.

C: I also want a fair market value for my trade-in, which would be $2,500.

S: I really don't think that's possible, but let me write that down, too.

C: Regarding the down payment, I'll be able to come up with $2,500, if you use my trade-in. I don't want to put down any cash.

S: Well, we'll see.

C: With $2,500 as the down payment, please quote the total price of the car and the monthly payment. Figure the price with and without the extended service contract, air-conditioning, roof rack, power sun roof, and pinstriping, and give me the price for each of those items. I also need to see payments for thirty-six, forty-eight, and sixty months. Also, what is your interest rate? That will do for now. Take my offer to your manager.

(The *customer* is now using the assumptive approach, valuing the trade at his price of $2,500. He then requests the total price of the car and the monthly payments because they both matter. The customer also wants to know how aftermarket items affect the price of the car. By asking for different loan terms, the customer is taking away the salesperson's bumping options.)

S: No problem, you're the boss.

C: Thanks.

(After a short absence the salesperson returns.)

S: My manager says your figures are unrealistic, but we're close. Also, we can still only offer you $1,500 for your trade.

C: I know my car is worth $2,500, because before coming here today I had it booked out at my bank. I've also looked at the newspapers and this car is selling for even more than $2,500.

(It is important to tell the dealer how you arrived at a certain figure. They want to make sure you know what you're talking about.)

S: Let me show you why it's only worth $1,500. Follow me.

(As the salesperson goes to the trade and picks out the problems, you must be ready with responses to justify your figure.)

C: The tires only have 5,000 miles, the engine has been very well maintained, and I just had a tune up. The front end is in good condition, and the car has never been in an accident. The problems you claim exist can be fixed for very little money. Also, other cars like mine have worn-out carpet and faded paint but they are selling for $2,500.

S: OK. But with only the trade-in as the down payment, we'll need a monthly payment of $340 per month, for forty-eight months.

C: I can't afford that, it's just too high. I can go up to $260 for forty-eight months.

S: Well, that doesn't sound right, but let me talk to my manager.

(During this absence, the salesperson's discussion with the manager goes something like this:)

S: I can't get this guy off $2,500 on the trade, and he insists on no cash down and $260 per month for forty-eight months.

M: Well, we appraised the trade at $2,500, too. That's the actual cash value. We were offering $1,500, to make $1,000 on the trade. So, if he absolutely must have the actual cash value for his car, bump him to sixty months and we'll make the deal. ($260 for sixty months equals a total payment of $15,600.)

S: I'll offer sixty months at $300, and if he fights I'll go down a few dollars at a time, stopping at $260.

M: That's excellent!

(The salesperson now returns to the customer.)

S: Well, with only your trade as down payment, we can do it at $300 per month for sixty months.

(This bump is an important one. The additional twelve monthly payments adds thousands of dollars to the cost of the deal.)

C: Sixty-month financing is fine with me, but only at $210 per month.

(You should go up only a few dollars at a time until the salesperson says he has made his final offer. This is how you discover the dealer's bottom-line price on the deal. This dealer may want more than $260 because they are not "stealing" $1,000 on your trade, but other dealers will accept a "slim" deal rather than no deal at all.)

S: That simply cannot be done. I can go down to . . . (He states different numbers each time you come up a few dollars. If you've been to other dealers and know their bottom line is $260, you can stop at $255 and see if he accepts the deal.)

S: The absolute bottom line is $260 per month for sixty months.

C: Is that your final offer?

S: Yes, it is.

C: Put it on a purchase order and I'll go talk to my bank.

If this is the first or second dealership visited, do not buy. If you get a purchase order, take it to other dealerships and your bank, to find money at a lower rate than dealer-arranged financing. If the dealer refuses to give a purchase order, at least you know their best offer. Then, go to other dealers and tell them you were offered these terms.

This example shows how important it is to be prepared and have compared prices at the various dealerships. (The "winning" car buyer saved $25 per month – $1,500 over the term of the car.) When it comes to striking a final deal, it is vital that you maintain control of the buying situation, that you stick to the picture you created, and that you get the deal that suits YOU and your budget.

The deal you achieve after negotiating discounts, agreeing on the down payment, monthly payments, and trade-in allowance is, *at that time,* the "best deal" available from that dealership. (As we said earlier, the scramble for monthly commission bonuses may sweeten a deal at the end of the month just before closing time.) It may not, however, be the best deal around. That's why you check other dealer-ships.

No Money Down

Perhaps you have heard of car buying with no money down. Unfortunately, that is rare. Sales tax and license fees are due immediately, whether you finance through the dealer or your own bank. Occasionally dealers pay these fees and add them back into the selling price. Moreover, the less money you put down on the car, the greater amount you'll have to pay in finance charges on that bigger loan.

Also, to qualify for no money down (that is, no down payment *in addition to* tax and fees) you need very strong credit. The weaker a buyer's credit rating, the larger the down payment. For many consumers, the "no money down" claim turns out to be a gimmick.

Your Trade-in

Negotiations usually begin on the topic of trade-ins (selling your present car to the dealer to offset part of the purchase price), because the value of the trade-in greatly affects the deal. There are many ways dealers play with the finances of a deal when a trade exists. For example, there are profits or losses made on trade-ins (which can increase or decrease the cost of the new car), and trade-ins can increase down payments.

The goal, if you have a trade, is to get the actual cash value of your car. The industry standard in most of the United States for assessing its value is the *Kelley Blue Book*. Other books—like NADA (National Automobile Dealer's Association) in the East—serve the same purpose in other areas. You can find the book at banks and some libraries as well as car dealerships. Before going to the dealer, find out the value of your car so you can deal from a position of equal knowledge.

The *Blue Book,* updated every two months, gives two prices for each car, wholesale and retail. Dealers do not offer the retail value for trade-ins because they plan to resell the car at a profit. Instead, they initially offer wholesale value or less, and then deduct reconditioning costs. Accepting their first offer guarantees lots of profit for the dealer. You must negotiate to get a fair price for your trade.

Reconditioning means replacing or fixing anything on the trade-in to ready it for resale. Be prepared for the dealer to overstate the extent of reconditioning necessary as well as the cost of the repairs. But body dents, worn tires, and mechanical problems will decrease the value of your trade. Anticipate the items the dealer will say need repairs and have an idea of the cost of the repair. Your preparation will help ensure a fair price from the dealer for your trade-in.

Dealers usually do not increase their offer on the trade-in for such items as expensive stereos, seat covers, and fancy paint jobs installed by the customer. Therefore, remove whatever optional equipment you can before giving up the trade-in. That stereo will sound even better in your new car.

Sometimes the value of your trade-in is high enough to serve as the only form of down payment: if you own the car free and clear (you've paid off your car loan), or have a loan balance less than the value of the car. The difference between the amount owed and the trade-in value (called equity) can be applied to the down payment.

Usually, the required down payment will exceed the value of the trade. For example, if your trade is worth $2,000 but the required down payment is $3,000, the dealer will want $1,000 cash in addition to the trade. But like everything else on the lot, the amount of the down payment and the value of the trade are negotiable. Push to get fair value for your trade and to have it accepted as the entire down payment.

When negotiating the trade-in, the first item you encounter is the dealer's appraisal pad. This note pad is used to detail various information on the trade, such as the mileage, equipment, and the vehicle's general condition. Based on the appraisal, the dealership will make an offer. As we said, the first figure will be low. They hope you accept this figure without negotiating; if you do, they make extra money.

Have your old car appraised at several dealerships. Each will probably offer a different figure. Just because one dealership offers more money does not necessarily mean you are getting a better overall deal. Chances are that the dealers offering more for the trade are giving an over-allowance to let the customer believe he is getting a great price for the trade. The dealer simply adds the difference between the actual cash value of the trade-in and the extra amount paid to the customer to the sale price of the new car. This trick is one of many that dealers can play when a trade is part of a deal.

Sometimes customers want to trade their cars before paying off their loans. To illustrate this, suppose Ms. Hall owns a two-year-old car on which she still owes $10,000. Unfortunately, the best trade-in offer she can get for the car is $7,000. That's a $3,000 difference, for which Ms. Hall is responsible. The dealer may split this difference to make a sale and offer Ms. Hall $8,500. Once again, the new car profits compensate for the losses on the over-allowance.

If you're not satisfied with the price that any dealer

offers, you can sell your own used car. By selling the car yourself, you'll receive a price closer to the retail book value. You'll have to balance this potential cash bonus against the work required to earn it. You have to advertise the car, return phone calls from shoppers, and spend time giving test drives. Perhaps most important, unless you have a transportation alternative, you'll have to wait until you take delivery of your new car. That means you won't have the proceeds of the sale available for your down payment. Check the classified ads in local papers to see the price of your car on the market, keeping in mind that most sales are made below the advertised price. If the advertised prices aren't considerably higher than your best trade offer, you're probably better off doing the trade-in.

The Credit Application

After discussing your trade-in, the salesperson turns to the credit application, which the dealer calls a "Customer Statement." The dealer immediately checks your application with a credit rating bureau, such as TRW or Trans Union. This process provides your credit rating. If you have good credit, they want to sell you the car *now* so that you don't have time to reconsider or shop around.

If you want to arrange the financing through your bank or credit union, hoping to get a lower rate, tell the salesperson. The dealer will nevertheless ask for your credit history, seeking a possible one pay contract (discussed later in this chapter).

Continuing to use the assumptive approach, the salesperson will ask how you want "your new car" registered. Registration consists of your name, address, city, state, and zip code as well as the new car information. Remember, giving this information does not commit you to buy.

Discounts

If you pay the sticker price for a car, you've paid too much. Discounts are a widespread practice at every dealership, but no one's going to offer them to you. You have to *ask* for discounts – and it's your right to ask, so go for it!

A realistic discount is a minimum of 10% off the manufacturer's sticker price, so ask for 30%. Similarly, ask for at least 20% to 40% off the aftermarket items shown on the dealer's addendum sticker, in hopes of getting 10% to 30% off. Remember, the addendum sticker is the dealership's way of making lots of extra profit.

Your Offer

Consider the sticker price and the dealer's offer and make an offer on the new car. Take 30% off the sticker price – and don't be discouraged when the salesperson tells you you're crazy.

An offer to purchase the car at a big discount is considered more seriously if you back it up with a partial cash offer and a willingness to buy the car right away. Show the salesperson $500 or more, tell him you will take the car home now, and big discounts are much more likely. Of course, only use this strategy when you are really ready to buy the car now!

Occasionally the dealership wants a deposit to hold the car, pending credit approval. This deposit is refundable at any time. They want to remove you from the market so that you'll stop shopping around and buy from them. Before giving a deposit make sure you have come to terms on the price of the car and on aftermarket items such as extended service contracts, alarms, pinstriping, luggage racks, paint sealant (also called paint undercoat), and special wheels.

The salesperson may ask to take your trade-in keys, or your registration slip, or your money, into the manager's office to present your offer to the sales manager. Under no circumstances give them your keys, documents, or money until the deal is final. Once the dealer has your keys or money he has leverage over you. During negotiations, confrontations sometimes occur between customer and salesperson. The irate customer walks out, gets into his car . . . but where are the keys? That's right – they are in the manager's office! Guess what? The customer returns, embarrassed, forced to beg to get back his own keys. Now the dealer has a second opportunity to sell the car.

To take control of the buying situation, tell the salesperson how much you want the down payment and monthly payments to be. The salesperson will probably say your figures are unrealistic. He is trying to bump you up into a larger down payment and/or higher monthly payments.

Remember, it's all part of the negotiating process. Ask the salesperson to take your figures to the sales manager. The salesperson presents the sales manager with a work sheet, including information about your trade (the appraisal pad), the price of the new car, your offer, the salesperson's requested down payment and monthly payment, and your registration information. Remember, the salesperson cannot guarantee a price, only the sales manager can.

The Give and Take

The dealer knows that the monthly payment is generally the most important part of the deal for the customer. Therefore, when the salesperson returns, he usually presents only the dealer's proposed monthly payment. This monthly payment includes the car, interest, sales tax, license fees, and probably many high-profit aftermarket items. By getting you to focus on the monthly payment, the dealer is hiding the total cost of the car. DON'T FALL FOR IT! Even if you can afford the monthly payment proposed, negotiate each part of the deal. Focus on the total price of the new car and the value of your trade-in. Price each aftermarket item, and remember to ask for those discounts!

Since the dealer cannot trick you into focusing on the monthly payment, they will switch to alternative tactics. For example, they may offer a huge monthly payment for a short term. They are trying to scare you back into their payment. When you object, the dealer will switch to a smaller payment for a longer term.

They may also seek to remove the air-conditioning and other features from the car. Negotiate each aftermarket item, but do not remove the ones you really want. For example, take money off the extended service contract, remove the car alarm and pinstriping. Beware: if you still cannot agree, they will try to bump you to a less expensive car. Nevertheless, do not be swayed from the car you really want until you are convinced, by more than one dealer, that it is simply not available at your price.

Check local stores for their prices on special paint jobs, stereos, special wheels, and other aftermarket items. Specialty stores usually charge less than the dealer does. In addition to saving money on the items, you'll also lower the cost of driving the car off the lot. That's less to finance and a lower total price for the new vehicle.

Another popular sales tactic is to wear you down. If the dealer keeps pushing for "just another few dollars a month," many customers will give in, because they are tired and just want to get it over with. If you are tired, get up and walk away. Those extra few dollars add up to hundreds over the life of the loan.

You have now made your offers (total price, trade-in, down payment, and monthly payment), and the dealer has counter-offered. At this point in the negotiations you should know if you have a deal or are close enough to continue negotiating.

How do you know whether you are close? Before you sat down, you should have known what you wanted to pay as the total price of the car, the down payment, and the monthly payment, and for how many months you wanted to finance your loan. Look at the dealer's numbers and compare them to your own. If you are far away, keep negotiating, until the dealer has made his final offer.

Purchase Orders

When you have the dealer's final offer, you are at a critical moment. You have done everything to get the car you want, on your terms. You have overcome all the dealer's tricks. Get their final offer on a purchase order.

Purchase orders prove you can buy "this car" for "this price." You are only getting a commitment from the dealer for the price they offered; you have not agreed to buy a car. Make sure the purchase order lists everything you have negotiated, including aftermarket items.

There are times when a purchase order is given to a customer, but the manager has not signed it. Unless signed by the sales manager, the dealer is not bound. Remember, get a signed purchase order, then you have a firm price. NO VERBAL AGREEMENTS! You'll need a signed purchase order to finance the car through a bank or credit union.

You'll also want to take the signed purchase order to

other dealers. Find out if they can beat this deal. Remember that other dealers want a sale NOW. They will pressure you to buy now if they promise to beat that price. Ask them, "By how much will you beat it?" When they answer, offer hundreds of dollars less. When they have made their final offers, say, "Thank you very much," and leave.

A signed purchase order from each dealer you visit would be ideal, but dealers usually refuse. They're not dumb, they know what you are doing, and they don't want their purchase order taken down the block to the next dealer. Therefore, take your purchase order elsewhere and use this tactic again. Also, you can verbally tell a dealer what another dealer offered, even if you couldn't get a purchase order. This makes it easy to locate the best deal available.

If one of the later dealers, who didn't give you a signed purchase order, offers the best deal, you may have trouble getting that same deal again. Because they didn't give you a purchase order, they're not bound to live up to the verbal offer they made. Find the salesperson you spoke with originally and remind him of the offer. Most of the time, he'll be anxious enough to make the sale to go along with the quoted price. BEWARE OF REOPENING NEGOTIATIONS! Insist on the quoted price or take a walk. Without a signed purchase order, you have no other choices.

Shop as many dealers as your time and patience permit, but you must visit at least three to get any idea of the best deal available. Remember, you can always go back.

It is possible that no dealer will sell the car on your terms. If this happens, rethink your strategy. For example, consider offering a larger down payment, extending the term of the loan, or buying a less expensive car.

You will never know exactly how much profit the dealer

is making on your sale because there are many ways they make money: on the financing, on the aftermarket accessories, on the trade-in, on the basic sale price, and on rebates from the manufacturer. Instead of concentrating on how much "they are making off me," winning car buyers should think about how much "I am saving."

The One Pay Contract

If the salesperson finds that you're a good credit risk, you may be offered a one pay contract (also called an either/or contract). Under the one pay, you receive a set number of days, usually seven, to arrange your own financing. The one pay contract gives the buyer a chance to find a lower interest rate at a bank or elsewhere.

Signing a one pay contract means you agree to buy that particular car and take it home now. You have definitely bought *that* car. The only question is who will provide the financing, you or the dealer.

Remember that deals often occur on Saturdays, Sundays, and holidays, when banks and finance companies are closed. The dealer is taking a risk, putting a car in the possession of a total stranger, based on the expectation of financing the deal. Therefore, one pay contracts are only given to people with good credit, when the dealer is convinced that the customer can be financed.

The buyer is taking an even bigger risk than the dealer. The one pay contract carries a high dealer-financed interest rate (usually 18%) in the event that you're unable to find other financing. The dealer hopes the time passes before you've found alternative financing – this would force you to "cash in your contract" and would bind you to that high interest rate. If you are just one day late, YOU LOSE. And if you try to refinance the new car, that rate may be even higher, because in the bank's opinion you have a used car.

If a one pay contract occurs, the dealer has won. If the customer walks away with only a purchase order, leaving no money and no commitment to buy, the customer has won. A purchase order gives the customer a tool to get better deals, by "shopping" the purchase order around town.

Summary:

1. During the negotiations, you are not committed to buy the car. Don't feel pressured.
2. Asking for discounts is your right. THINK BIG.
3. Unless you have very strong credit, you will not qualify for "no money down."
4. Know the *Blue Book* value of your trade-in. Try to get the actual cash value.
5. More money on the trade-in does not necessarily mean you are getting a better overall deal.
6. If you have good credit the dealer wants you to take the car home *now,* so you do not have a chance to reconsider your deal.
7. The salesperson cannot guarantee a price; only the sales manager can.
8. Focus on the total price of the car, not the monthly payment, which allows the dealer to hide the total cost. Negotiate each part of the deal separately, including the trade, down payment, interest rate, and monthly payment. (Know beforehand what you want each of these to be.)
9. When the dealer has made their final offer, get a signed purchase order to confirm "that car" at "that price." NO VERBAL AGREEMENTS!

10. A one pay contract means the customer has definitely bought the car; the only question is who will provide the financing, customer or dealer. A signed purchase order is better for the customer than a one pay contract.

7   *The Last Step*

The Finance Manager

If your negotiations succeeded to this point and you have settled on price and terms, you are still not finished. Why? You have not done the legal paperwork involved in buying a car. For the final arrangements, you are now introduced to the finance manager.

Recognize that you are saying you will buy *this car now*. If you are not ready to buy now, you should not be in the finance manager's office. Get out.

The finance manager's major responsibilities are to arrange financing, do the legal paperwork, and have you sign on the dotted line. He also tries to sell whatever aftermarket items you avoided during earlier negotiations, such as alarms, tinted windows, and pinstriping. In other words, the dealership gets a second chance to sell you unwanted extras!

The primary aftermarket item sold by the finance manager is the extended service contract. When negotiating, a reasonable discount is 33%. So, ask for 50% in hopes of getting 33% to 50% off. Remember, aftermarket items are the dealership's way of making lots of extra profit.

Extended Service Contracts

Extended service contracts should not be confused with warranties. A warranty means that the manufacturer is responsible to fix specified parts of the car, at little or no deductible to you, for a specified period of time. This is the "5/50 Protection Plan" advertised by many car makers. (The 5/50 means the warranty applies for five years or 50,000 miles, whichever comes first.) Many warranties are written to exclude everything except the engine and transmission. Even so-called "bumper to bumper" warranties should be carefully examined for excluded parts and services.

The extended service contract covers items that the manufacturer's warranty excludes, as well as warranty items after the warranty expires. It protects against the cost of unexpected major breakdowns, at home or while traveling. Under the manufacturer's warranty, you can have the car serviced at any dealership (of the same make), no matter where it was purchased. Unfortunately, extended service contracts are not universally accepted; a dealer may not participate in all extended service contract programs that are generally available. Therefore, get a list of participating dealers if you buy an extended service contract.

Many extended service contracts are written to exclude work owners need most often. Consider which extended service contract best fits your driving needs, and understand that not all repairs will be covered. If you do your own repairs or enjoy tinkering with cars, you probably do not want an extended service contract. If you know little about repairs, you may want the most extensive coverage available.

Also, not all extended service contracts are equal in quality. Here's a list of suggested items for coverage: engine, transmission, rear-wheel drive, front-wheel drive, or four-wheel drive (whichever applies), radiator, steering, front suspension, electrical system, air-conditioning. Everyday wear and tear items such as brake pads, tires, and clutch (if you have a manual transmission) are usually not covered under the contract.

When the dealership sells an extended service contract, they are usually acting as an agent for another company, called the warranty company. Anything over the dealership's cost of the contract is the dealer's profit.

Remember, the extended service contract is an aftermarket item, intended to make money for the dealer and warranty company. When a consumer has warranty work done, the dealership performing the work gets paid by the warranty company. The contract may also require the consumer to use the authorized dealers for all maintenance, including checkups at specified times, such as 7,500 miles and 15,000 miles. If you do not follow the contract requirements, the dealer may not honor it.

Insurance

Unless you pay cash for a car, thereby owning it outright, you need proof of auto insurance before driving the car off the lot. In some states you must be insured even if you buy outright.

If the buyer does not have insurance and wants the car immediately, the dealer must arrange for temporary insurance, at the customer's cost. If the dealer allows an uninsured car off the property and there is an accident, the dealer is responsible.

It is generally less expensive to buy insurance directly from an insurance agent, without dealer participation. If you do not have insurance, arrange it before taking delivery of the car. This takes only an hour or two and will save much money. Remember, insurance through the dealer is another high-priced aftermarket item.

Temporary insurance through the dealer is called an insurance binder. The dealership is an agent of one or more insurance companies. The binder gives you temporary, immediate insurance. The insurance binder rates vary according to the selling price of the car; the typical charge for a thirty-day binder is $100–200.

A life insurance policy is also available through the dealership. If the buyer dies, the insurance company pays off the loan balance – no matter how large – for the named beneficiaries. The policy differs from conventional life insurance in that only the car is paid off. There are no other benefits of regular life insurance policies, such as payments of cash to the named beneficiaries.

A disability insurance policy is also available through the dealership. If you become disabled, the disability insurance makes your monthly payments. Generally, disability insurance does not take effect until fifteen days of disability have passed. As with the life insurance mentioned above, the dealer's policy pays no cash to you, it only makes the car payment.

Life and disability insurance can be financed and included in your monthly payment, or they can be purchased separately through an insurance company. Remember, they're high-profit aftermarket items for the dealer.

The Dotted Line

After the finance manager has finished trying to sell you all the aftermarket items, he presents the paperwork to finish the deal. The typical paperwork involved in the purchase of a car is:

Motor Vehicle Contract. The written agreement between customer and dealership on the vehicle selling price. Make sure the vehicle identification number on this contract matches the identification number on the car.

Power of Attorney. The customer authorizes the dealership to do the paperwork required by the state's Department of Motor Vehicles. This service usually costs $25. The dealer does only DMV work, so you're not signing your life away. Some people do the paperwork themselves, saving a few dollars but buying a trip to the DMV.

Odometer Statement. The dealership states that to the best of their knowledge, the odometer has not been tampered with and the mileage reading is true.

Bill of Sale. This document attests the sale of your trade-in (if any) to the dealer.

Report of Sale. The dealer sends this document to the Department of Motor Vehicles to register your new car.

Proof of Insurance.

Driver's License. (If not of the buyer, then of the person driving off the lot.)

Extended Service Contract (if purchased).

Summary:
1. You should not be in the finance manager's office if you are not ready to buy *now*.
2. The finance manager's function is to sell whatever aftermarket items you avoided during earlier negotia-

tions, arrange the financing, and do the legal paperwork.

3. An extended service contract should not be confused
with a manufacturer's warranty.

4. Extended service contracts cover the car after the
manufacturer's warranty expires, plus items not included in the warranty.

5. Unless you are paying cash, you need proof of auto
insurance before driving the car home.

6. Life and disability insurance are also available
through the dealer. These policies pay no cash, they
only make the car payments.

7. Life and disability insurance can be financed and included in the monthly payment, or can be purchased
separately through an insurance company.

8   *Before Taking Delivery*

Inspection

You've signed on the dotted line for your picture-perfect car. You are ready to drive it home, but you notice there is a dent or broken headlight. Maybe the damage was not there a little while ago, but it is now. Before you drive your new car home, remember to check carefully for any physical damage.

Do not let your excitement blind you into taking damaged goods! If the dealer says "bring it back tomorrow and we'll fix it," refuse. Simply say you will take the car when it is fixed. Be sure the manager signs a statement agreeing to fix the car at a specified time.

Also, make sure a gas cap, owner's manual, and cigarette lighter are included. Check the inside and outside lights. Do not be surprised if there is very little gasoline. A polite request to "fill 'er up" is generally honored.

Lemon Laws

.   Some states impose special consumer protection laws on car makers, commonly called "lemon laws." Lemon laws (the details vary from state to state) give consumers the right to a replacement or refund for cars with major, chronic problems.

The owner has to prove certain things are wrong with the car to make it a legal "lemon," such as chronic problems with an essential system (such as transmission or steering), or several problems with different parts. There is usually a strict time period (for example, the first year) within which these problems must occur in order to qualify as a "lemon." Consult an attorney for the detailed requirements in your state.

Summary:
1. Check the car for physical damage before driving off the lot.
2. Make sure that any promises made are in writing.
3. Some states have "lemon laws." Consult an attorney in your state if you have chronic problems with your new car.

9   *Buying a Used Car*

The Mechanic's Inspection

The key to buying a used car is to have a mechanic inspect the vehicle before purchase. If possible, the mechanic should specialize in that specific make of car, but any mechanic is better than none at all.

Here is a list of items that should be inspected by your mechanic:

Engine. Check all fluids, points, condenser, rotor, spark plugs, and ignition wire. Look for oil leaks, transmission fluid leaks, and power steering fluid leaks. Check the belts, air-conditioning, heater, and battery. Make sure the radiator does not leak and that all hoses are securely fastened.

Braking system. Check the calipers, brake pads, rotor, master cylinder, front disks (and/or rear disks), and drums.

Suspension. Check the condition of the shock absorbers, ball joints, tie rod ends, and idler arm. Look for uneven wear on inside or outside edges of tires; these are signs of suspension problems.

After the mechanic has completed the inspection, discuss the findings in detail. Ask about the mechanical reliability of the model in general. What parts of this car do you have to replace immediately? How long will other important parts last? For example, does the clutch need to be replaced immediately, or can you drive 20,000 miles? Does the engine need an overhaul in the immediate future, or can it last 50,000 miles?

Remember, any money spent on repair work increases the total cost of your used car and does not necessarily add to the resale value.

Be sure to take a test drive.

The Physical Appearance

If you are satisfied with the mechanic's report and test drive, then carefully examine the exterior and interior of the car. Check for body damage. See if the body appears smooth. If the body looks or feels uneven, it may be evidence of an accident. A difference in the paint usually indicates repaired body damage. If you see it, ask the seller for an explanation.

Remember to check for *frame damage,* since this greatly reduces the car's value. A damaged frame can cause excessive wear on tires, difficult steering, and generally poor performance. Once bent, a frame is difficult and costly to repair. A bent frame often causes insurance companies to declare a car a total loss.

Check mirrors, bumpers, and hub caps for cracks or missing parts. Also, inspect for rust corrosion, especially under the car. Rust build-up is generally found around the wheel wells and in the trunk area.

Check the tires: are they the same make, and are they all white walls or solid black? Replacing four tires and having them wheel balanced and mounted could cost at least $200. Figure that, and other repair costs, into the total price of the vehicle.

Carefully examine the interior of the car. What is the condition of the carpet? Is it worn out, or does it have holes? If there are seat covers, check underneath for torn upholstery. Is the dashboard cracking? Is the electrical system functioning? For example, do the horn, interior lights, headlights, and directional signals work?

Valuing the Car

If you're satisfied with your findings, the next step is to value the car. Remember, no two used cars are identical. Gather information about the used car you are considering—the year, make, model, mileage, and equipment (stereo, air-conditioning, type of transmission)—and call the bank to have the car booked out. As you will recall, having the car booked out means the bank finds the value as listed in the *Kelley Blue Book*. Remember, value is determined by mileage, equipment, and popularity of the car. Local newspapers and magazines also provide prices for used cars offered by private parties.

You can buy a used car through a private party or a dealership. If you can pay cash, consider buying from a private party, through the newspaper, or through friends and family. Their prices are usually lower than dealers'.

On the other hand, if something goes wrong with a privately bought car, the person who sold it may be gone, or refuse to talk about the problem. Legal action may be your only recourse. Buying through a dealer assures that someone will be there if a problem arises, plus extended service contracts and financing are available (though lenders do not usually finance cars older than five years). Negotiate with a dealer on a used car as you would on a new car. If you are careful and follow the steps discussed here, you have an excellent chance of getting a good car at the right price.

Summary:
1. Have a mechanic look at the car.
2. Carefully examine the exterior and interior.
3. Know the car's book value before negotiating the price.

10   *Leasing*

Leasing vs. Buying

Leasing is an alternative way of paying for an automobile. Strange as it may sound, credit requirements are stricter for leasing than for buying. Leasing usually requires less of an initial cash outlay in exchange for possession of an expensive automobile, which explains the stricter credit requirements.

Leasing has other benefits: the customer can change cars frequently without having to sell the old car, can drive a "loaner car" while servicing the leased vehicle, and may also receive tax benefits. For example, if the vehicle is for business purposes, some portion of the total lease payment becomes tax deductible. For further information about tax advantages, check with your accountant.

How Does a Lease Work?

Leasing companies, called lessors, are middlemen. They borrow from banks (or use their own money) and buy cars from dealerships.

They make their profit by marking up the cost of the car, the interest rate, and the aftermarket items. The lease payment consists of monthly depreciation (the car's loss of value because of use), interest, and taxes.

To illustrate this, suppose Miss Wenger wants to lease a 1987 Ford and use it for business purposes. She visits a leasing company. The company buys that car from a dealer for $12,000, the best price available. The company borrows the $12,000 from a bank at 8% interest, then charges $13,000 for the car. When calculating the lease payment, 16% interest is charged. Leasing is a very profitable industry!

When the Lease Ends

Customers, called lessees, do not pay off their loans to $0 like car owners. There is an unpaid balance called the residual value. This is the unpaid portion of the car's value, projected when the lease was written. It's the difference between the original capitalized cost of the vehicle, including the profit of the lessor, and the depreciation of that cost at the end of the lease. For example, on a $10,000 car for a three-year lease, with the car projected to be worth $5,500 at the end of the lease, the residual value is $4,500. Payments are based on the amount of depreciation ($5,500) and the cost to operate the lease (a service charge similar to interest). The depreciated amount is credited on each monthly payment. If at the end of the three-year lease the car is valued at $6,500 in the market, you can either buy or sell it and keep the $1,000 difference. However, if the car has a market value of $5,000 at the end of the lease, you would owe the $500 difference. Or, as many lessees do, you can trade the vehicle in to the lessor for a new car.

Leases typically run twenty-four to sixty months and are called "open-ended" or "closed-ended," depending upon what options the lessee has when the lease ends.

Closed-ended lease. Closed-ended leases leave the leasing company with the car, and the driver with no car and no further obligation. If the lessee chooses to pay the residual value, however, he or she owns the car.

The lessee *is* responsible for damages above normal wear and tear, such as dents and broken glass. There can also be a charge for "excessive mileage," as defined in the lease, which can be costly. Negotiate the mileage limitation!

Monthly payments are higher with closed-ended leases; this is the lessor's way of minimizing their potential loss of profit if the residual value is less than originally projected, or if the lessee chooses not to buy the car.

Open-ended lease. The driver has the option to buy at lease end, but must pay part of the residual value, whether keeping the car or giving it back. If the residual value is higher than the *Blue Book* value at lease end, the lessee is responsible for a part of that difference, as defined in the lease. Damages over normal wear and tear are also the lessee's responsibility. There is normally no charge for excessive mileage.

Regardless of lease type, the lessee is always responsible for regular maintenance, such as tune-ups, new tires, and oil changes.

Neither type of lease is necessarily better than the other. The monthly payment on a closed-ended lease is higher, but there is no further obligation at lease end. Mileage restrictions in closed-ended leases are negotiable, but higher mileage means a bigger monthly payment. Open-ended leases do not have mileage restrictions, but the customer may have to pay additional money at the end of the lease if the car's value is less than the residual value.

Choose the type of lease that best fits your needs. If you might want to keep the car, consider a closed-ended lease, as the residual will be lower than with an open-ended lease. If you know you won't keep the car, consider an open-ended lease (the monthly payments are lower and there are no mileage restrictions), especially if the car has good resale value. If the car's resale value is close to the residual value, you probably won't have to pay additional money at lease end.

Insurance Under a Lease

Car owners decide the amount, and the types, of insurance to buy. With bank loans, owners need only obtain collision coverage to protect the car, the bank's investment. Some states require liability insurance; check with your local Department of Motor Vehicles.

Under a lease the leasing company still owns the car; the driver is just using it. Therefore leasing companies require high insurance coverage, which increases the total cost of the lease.

Can I End the Lease Early?

Early termination of a lease, whether open- or closed-ended, usually carries penalties. Negotiate the early termination clause before signing a contract.

Alternatives to Leasing Companies

Many dealerships lease cars. Like leasing companies, dealers mark up the cost of the car and interest rates. Unlike leasing companies, dealers usually do not provide extra services, such as loan cars.

Banks lease cars, usually at the lowest rates, but they only accept the best credit risks. In exchange for their low rates, the rules are more rigid. For example, it is harder to end a bank lease early than other leases, and loan cars are not provided. Mileage restrictions may also apply and odd lease terms (like twenty-nine months) are not written.

Go to the bank directly before going to a leasing company or dealership. Leasing companies and dealerships are middlemen; if they arrange a bank lease, they will not pass the savings along to you but will keep the difference as added profit.

Leasing Used Cars

It is possible to lease used cars, although it is not common. Banks generally do not participate in this market, but some large leasing companies offer this option. People usually lease used cars in order to get a lower monthly payment.

Summary:
1. Down payments are smaller when leasing.
2. Leasing may carry tax advantages over buying.
3. Leasing allows drivers to change cars frequently.
4. High insurance is required on leased cars, adding to the cost.
5. Negotiate excessive mileage charges and early termination penalties.
6. Consider bank leasing first for the best price.

Conclusion

Car dealers take advantage of their knowledge and the customer's lack of knowledge. Remember, they will forget you five minutes after you leave. But you must live with the consequences of your choice. Be firm – you will get a better deal.

Finally, *if in doubt, do not buy.* Take time to think. You can always go back later!

Appendix: Financing Charts

These financing charts are created for the nonprofessional. If your interest rate is not listed here, you can go to a bookstore, bank, or credit union and obtain a financial guide for installment loans.

8³/4% Monthly Loan Payments

Loan Amount	One Year (12 months)	Two Years (24 months)	Three Years (36 months)	Four Years (48 months)	Five Years (60 months)
1,000	87.34	45.57	31.68	24.77	20.64
1,500	131.00	68.36	47.53	37.15	30.96
2,000	174.67	91.14	63.37	49.53	41.27
2,500	218.34	113.93	79.21	61.92	51.59
3,000	262.01	136.71	95.05	74.30	61.91
3,500	305.67	159.50	110.89	86.68	72.23
4,000	349.34	182.28	126.73	99.07	82.55
4,500	393.01	205.07	142.58	111.45	92.87
5,000	436.68	227.85	158.42	123.83	103.19
5,500	480.35	250.64	174.26	136.22	113.50
6,000	524.01	273.42	190.10	148.60	123.82
6,500	567.68	296.21	205.94	160.98	134.14
7,000	611.35	318.99	221.78	173.37	144.46
7,500	655.02	341.78	237.63	185.75	154.78
8,000	698.68	364.56	253.47	198.13	165.10
8,500	742.35	387.35	269.31	210.52	175.42
9,000	786.02	410.13	285.15	222.90	185.74
9,500	829.69	432.92	300.99	235.28	196.05
10,000	873.36	455.70	316.84	247.67	206.37
11,000	960.69	501.27	348.52	272.43	227.01
12,000	1,048.03	546.84	380.20	297.20	247.65
13,000	1,135.36	592.41	411.89	321.96	268.28
14,000	1,222.70	637.98	443.57	346.73	288.92
15,000	1,310.03	683.55	475.25	371.50	309.56
16,000	1,397.37	729.12	506.94	396.26	330.20
17,000	1,484.70	774.69	538.62	421.03	350.83
18,000	1,572.04	820.26	570.30	445.80	371.47
19,000	1,659.38	865.83	601.99	470.56	392.11
20,000	1,746.71	911.40	633.67	495.33	412.74
21,000	1,834.05	956.97	665.35	520.10	433.38
22,000	1,921.38	1,002.54	697.04	544.86	454.02
23,000	2,008.72	1,048.11	728.72	569.63	474.66
24,000	2,096.05	1,093.68	760.40	594.40	495.29
25,000	2,183.39	1,139.25	792.09	619.16	515.93

12³/₄% Monthly Loan Payments

Loan Amount	One Year (12 months)	Two Years (24 months)	Three Years (36 months)	Four Years (48 months)	Five Years (60 months)
1,000	89.20	47.42	33.57	26.70	22.63
1,500	133.80	71.14	50.36	40.06	33.94
2,000	178.40	94.85	67.15	53.41	45.25
2,500	223.00	118.56	83.93	66.76	56.56
3,000	267.60	142.27	100.72	80.11	67.88
3,500	312.20	165.99	117.51	93.46	79.19
4,000	356.80	189.70	134.29	106.81	90.50
4,500	401.40	213.41	151.08	120.17	101.81
5,000	446.00	237.12	167.87	133.52	113.13
5,500	490.60	260.83	184.66	146.87	124.44
6,000	535.20	284.55	201.44	160.22	135.75
6,500	579.80	308.26	218.23	173.57	147.06
7,000	624.40	331.97	235.02	186.93	158.38
7,500	669.00	355.68	251.80	200.28	169.69
8,000	713.60	379.40	268.59	213.63	181.00
8,500	758.20	403.11	285.38	226.98	192.32
9,000	802.80	426.82	302.16	240.33	203.63
9,500	847.40	450.53	318.95	253.68	214.94
10,000	892.00	474.24	335.74	267.04	226.25
11,000	981.20	521.67	369.31	293.74	248.88
12,000	1,070.40	569.09	402.88	320.44	271.50
13,000	1,159.60	616.52	436.46	347.15	294.13
14,000	1,248.80	663.94	470.03	373.85	316.75
15,000	1,338.00	711.37	503.60	400.55	339.38
16,000	1,427.20	758.79	537.18	427.26	362.00
17,000	1,516.40	806.22	570.75	453.96	384.63
18,000	1,605.60	853.64	604.33	480.66	407.26
19,000	1,694.80	901.07	637.90	507.37	429.88
20,000	1,784.00	948.49	671.47	534.07	452.51
21,000	1,873.20	995.91	705.05	560.78	475.13
22,000	1,962.40	1,043.34	738.62	587.48	497.76
23,000	2,051.60	1,090.76	772.19	614.18	520.38
24,000	2,140.80	1,138.19	805.77	640.89	543.01
25,000	2,230.00	1,185.61	839.34	667.59	565.63

16³/4% **Monthly Loan Payments**

Loan Amount	One Year (12 months)	Two Years (24 months)	Three Years (36 months)	Four Years (48 months)	Five Years (60 months)
1,000	91.09	49.32	35.53	28.73	24.72
1,500	136.63	73.98	53.29	43.09	37.08
2,000	182.17	98.64	71.06	57.45	49.44
2,500	227.72	123.31	88.82	71.81	61.80
3,000	273.26	147.97	106.59	86.18	74.16
3,500	318.80	172.63	124.35	100.54	86.51
4,000	364.34	197.29	142.11	114.90	98.87
4,500	409.89	221.95	159.88	129.27	111.23
5,000	455.43	246.61	177.64	143.63	123.59
5,500	500.97	271.27	195.41	157.99	135.95
6,000	546.52	295.93	213.17	172.36	148.31
6,500	592.06	320.59	230.93	186.72	160.67
7,000	637.60	345.26	248.70	201.08	173.03
7,500	683.15	369.92	266.46	215.44	185.39
8,000	728.69	394.58	284.23	229.81	197.75
8,500	774.23	419.24	301.99	244.17	210.11
9,000	819.78	443.90	319.76	258.53	222.47
9,500	865.32	468.56	337.52	272.90	234.82
10,000	910.86	493.22	355.28	287.26	247.18
11,000	1,001.95	542.54	390.81	315.98	271.90
12,000	1,093.03	591.87	426.34	344.71	296.62
13,000	1,184.12	641.19	461.87	373.44	321.34
14,000	1,275.21	690.51	497.40	402.16	346.06
15,000	1,366.29	739.83	532.93	430.89	370.78
16,000	1,457.38	789.16	568.45	459.61	395.49
17,000	1,548.46	838.48	603.98	488.34	420.21
18,000	1,639.55	887.80	639.51	517.07	444.93
19,000	1,730.64	937.12	675.04	545.79	469.65
20,000	1,821.72	986.44	710.57	574.52	494.37
21,000	1,912.81	1,035.77	746.10	603.24	519.09
22,000	2,003.90	1,085.09	781.63	631.97	543.80
23,000	2,094.98	1,134.41	817.15	660.69	568.52
24,000	2,186.07	1,183.73	852.68	689.42	593.24
25,000	2,277.15	1,233.06	888.21	718.15	617.96

Index

About the Author

Steve Ross is a ten-year veteran of automobile sales. He has spent thousands of hours pounding the pavement, and thousands of hours behind the desk, making deals. Mr. Ross has worked in leasing and managed dealerships: he is a true auto industry insider.

Some other titles from Stackpole Books

How to Buy a House
Clear, practical advice from actual home buyers.
by Cyrus A. Yoakam

Prospecting for Old Furniture
A guide to buying and restoring affordable antiques for your home.
by Don Marotta

Basic Projects in Wildlife Watching
Learn more about wild birds and animals through your own first-hand experience.
By Sam Fadala

Soft Paths
How to enjoy the wilderness without harming it.
by Bruce Hampton and David Cole

Body Moves
The relationship between psychology and exercise; how to choose the best form of exercise for any individual's needs.
by James Gavin, Ph.D.

A Proper Garden: On Perennials in the Border
A fresh, inspiring book on how to grow cottage gardens and formal mixed borders.
By Elisabeth Sheldon

Patchwork and Quilting
Materials and techniques for making traditional and modern quilts.
by Brigitte Staub-Wachsmuth

Dried Flower Ideas
How to capture and extend the life of flowers and create seasonal arrangements for all occasions.
by Hedi Probst-Reinhardt

The Barrier Islands
A photographic history of life on Hog, Cobb, Smith, Cedar, Parramore, Metompkin, and Assateague.
by Curtis J. Badger and Rick Kellam

Available at your local bookstore,
or for complete ordering information, write:

Stackpole Books
P.O. Box 1831
Harrisburg, PA 17105

For fast service, credit card users may call 1-800-READ-NOW
In Pennsylvania, call 717-234-5041